Find Your Balance

A Teen's Workbook for Mindfulness, Self-Care, and Navigating Change with Courage

C.J. Kindren

with Dr Sui H. Wong MD FRCP

© **Copyright 2024 - All rights reserved.**

The content contained within this book may not be reproduced, duplicated or transmitted without direct written permission from the author or the publisher.

Under no circumstances will any blame or legal responsibility be held against the publisher, or author, for any damages, reparation, or monetary loss due to the information contained within this book, either directly or indirectly.

Legal Notice:

This book is copyright protected. It is only for personal use. You cannot amend, distribute, sell, use, quote or paraphrase any part, or the content within this book, without the consent of the author or publisher.

Disclaimer Notice:

Please note the information contained within this document is for educational and entertainment purposes only. All effort has been executed to present accurate, up to date, reliable, complete information. No warranties of any kind are declared or implied. Readers acknowledge that the author is not engaged in the rendering of legal, financial, medical or professional advice. The content within this book has been derived from various sources. Please consult a licensed professional before attempting any techniques outlined in this book.

By reading this document, the reader agrees that under no circumstances is the author responsible for any losses, direct or indirect, that are incurred as a result of the use of the information contained within this document, including, but not limited to, errors, omissions, or inaccuracies.

© 2024 EBH Press : EBHpress.com

ISBN: 978-1-917353-42-7 (eBook), 978-1-917353-41-0 (Paperback),

978-1-917353-40-3 (Hardcover)

Table of Contents

INTRODUCTION 1

CHAPTER 1: INCREASING AWARENESS AND UNDERSTANDING MINDFUL LIVING FOR TEENS 7
- WHAT ARE EMOTIONS? 8
- HOW CAN I RECOGNIZE WHAT I'M FEELING? 11
- WHY DO I FEEL STRESSED? 13
- MY JOURNAL 18

CHAPTER 2: UNDERSTANDING THE POWER OF SELF-CARE AND CREATING PRODUCTIVE ROUTINES 21
- MY HABITS 22
  - *Time Habits* 23
  - *Spending Habits* 24
  - *Study Habits* 25
  - *Building a Goal* 26
- MY ROUTINES 29
  - *Instructions* 29
  - *Daily Tracker* 30
  - *Evaluating Your Results* 31
  - *Daily Planner* 31
- MY HEALTH 32
  - *Mental Health* 34
  - *Sleep Health* 35
  - *Physical Health* 35
  - *Nutritional Health* 36
  - *Your Results* 36
- MY JOURNAL 37

CHAPTER 3: GETTING ORGANIZED FOR PRESENT AND FUTURE SUCCESS 39
- DAILY MINDFULNESS 40
- FOLLOWING A BUDGET 42
  - *Budget Template* 43
- TEEN ACCOUNTABILITY 44
- MY JOURNAL 47

CHAPTER 4: FOSTERING SELF-LOVE AND BOOSTING EMPOWERMENT WITH CONFIDENCE 49
- MY OWN BEST FRIEND 50
  - *Letter Through Time* 50

- *Thank You Note* 51
- *Good Friend, Bad Friend* 51
- THE POWER OF AFFIRMATIONS 52
  - *Negative Affirmations* 53
  - *Neutral Statements* 53
  - *Positive Affirmations* 54
- BIRD'S-EYE VIEW 55
  - *My Story* 55
  - *Third Person* 57
- MY JOURNAL 58

CHAPTER 5: NAVIGATING RELATIONSHIPS AND MANAGING YOUR SOCIAL LIFE 61

- SURVIVING SCHOOL 62
  - *Mindfulness Toolkit Guidelines* 62
- FOUNDATIONAL FRIENDSHIPS 63
  - *Communication Tips* 64
- HAPPY AT HOME 66
- MY JOURNAL 67

BONUS: 21-DAY ACTION PLAN 69

- WEEK ONE: UNLOCK YOUR MIND 69
  - *Daily To-Dos* 70
  - *Weekly Reflections* 71
- WEEK TWO: AMPLIFY YOUR POWER 72
  - *Daily To-Dos* 72
  - *Weekly Reflections* 73
- WEEK THREE: PRACTICE, PRACTICE, PRACTICE! 74
  - *Daily To-Dos* 74
  - *Weekly Reflections* 75
- FINAL THOUGHTS 76

CONCLUSION 77

YOUR VOICE CAN CHANGE LIVES 79

- KEEPING THE MINDFULNESS MOVEMENT GROWING! 79

REFERENCES 81

- IMAGE REFERENCES 83

Introduction

What do you like most about being a teen? The excitement of meeting different people? Learning about interesting topics in class? Or maybe new freedoms, like having a car or phone.

Despite this being an exciting time of your life, there are plenty of stressful challenges you deal with. Maybe your parents don't seem to understand you, your teachers are strict, or your friends have been flaky lately. Perhaps that person you have a crush on won't follow you back on social media, or you have no idea what you want to do when you grow up.

There's no limit to how many stressful, scary, or frustrating things you're dealing with now. It can feel like the weight of the world is falling on you when all you're trying to do is remember your locker combination!

Don't fret. The teenage years *can* be everything you've dreamed of—and then some.

What's the key to keeping it all together in the storm of adolescence? Mindfulness.

Mindfulness is a powerful state of awareness. What does that mean? This helps clear your mind so all those stressful thoughts start making a little more sense. It's a method of slowing down, and practicing different mental exercises to help it feel like you're reprogramming your brain!

When stress is ignored, it keeps growing, increasing the chance of developing mental illnesses such as stress and anxiety.

Anxiety disorders are common, with at least 8% of teens and children affected (Katzenstein, n.d.).

Additionally, these numbers only represent those teens who go to doctors and get diagnosed—many people are left struggling alone!

From the emotional impact of bullying to the pressure of picking a career path and college plan, you are presented with a never-ending supply of stress. Don't suffer alone anymore! Discover the power of mindfulness and how it can change your life for the better.

Mindfulness isn't something that happens with a quick snap of your fingers. However, it's not an overly complicated process either. With this step-by-step guide, you will incorporate small bits of mindfulness into daily life.

Whether you are a parent who sees your child struggling, a teacher who wants to encourage mindfulness, or a teen yourself who is facing problems at school or at home, there are many benefits of mindfulness for emotional management to be discovered throughout this book!

The upcoming activities in these chapters are geared toward teens, but all ages can benefit from a little more awareness. Mindfulness is a practical approach to living in the present, and practicing mindfulness can help anyone build a solid coping plan to handle stress.

In addition, these awareness exercises can help boost focus and attention so you can do better in school and make fewer impulsive decisions.

The book is structured around five skills:

1. Self-awareness to help with observing oneself and describing emotions.

2. Self-care as a way to be kind to yourself and create an environment that allows for daily mindfulness.

3. Self-management for managing reactions and fostering openness and curiosity.

4. Self-love as a way of being nonjudgmental.

5. Self-regulation to allow for more peace and joy in our lives.

These skills will help you explore some of the key qualities of mindfulness and turn them into a more practical application for daily life. The focus of these activities is to make mindfulness easier to understand.

By exploring, nurturing, and growing these skills, you can learn to be more present in the moment and incorporate mindfulness daily. Everything you need to get started lies in the pages ahead, but if you want to take mindfulness exploration even further, remember to check out the companion book to this one!

Additionally, there will be space to write throughout the workbook, but whether you are reading a physical or eBook copy, consider using an empty notebook to help record thoughts and expand on some of the activities throughout. You can also use a notebook so you can do these activities two, three, four, or even more times to make the most of your practice.

Take the activities at your own pace and remember mindfulness builds over time, so the best results will be seen in the future when you can look back on chronic stress as a thing of the past.

Discover all that mindfulness has to offer and move forward with the dedication to make the most of these mindfulness-boosting activities!

****

"A journey of a thousand miles, begins with a single step" – Lao Tzu

Chapter 1:
Increasing Awareness and Understanding Mindful Living for Teens

Mindfulness begins when an effort is made to be more aware. Why is this important? It helps your brain become stronger so you can let go of all those thoughts you don't want, and focus more on thoughts you do want!

The teenage years are a pivotal time, which means that a lot of important milestones are happening. By learning how to keep a strong mindset, it becomes easier to conquer stress and feel better!

> **Did You Know?**
>
> - Feeling stress is normal and your body has built-in functions that start automatically when you sense danger.
>
> - Chronic stress can affect your immune system and could even cause digestive problems (Stress, n.d.).
>
> - Studies show that mindfulness improves your ability to deal with emotions (Roemer, 2015).

Reaching a state of mindfulness is something we can achieve with emotional management. This starts by recognizing that we are experiencing an emotion or feeling. Once we start labeling our emotions, it becomes easier to put how we're feeling into words and actions, therefore identifying stress and reducing its effects in the process.

What Are Emotions?

How are you feeling? The first word that comes to mind might be an emotion, like happy, nervous, or curious. Emotions aren't just mental states, either. Have you ever been so happy you couldn't help but jump, or so nervous you couldn't help but shake?

Emotions are powerful and often control our thoughts and behavior. On top of this, we don't always realize we are experiencing an emotion. What ends up happening is that we might take action on an emotion without thinking about the effects of that action. This describes impulsivity—and impulsive actions often have consequences that add even more stress to what we're already feeling.

One way to ensure we stay on top of our feelings and emotions is by labeling them. When you do this, it becomes easier to take a step back, think clearly, and take a better and more productive action in response to that emotion.

Research from the last few years shows that more than one in three teens struggle with stress (Mandriota, 2022). Take a moment to think about your circle of friends. If one in three are experiencing stress, a lot of people you know are likely feeling the same things as you!

Stress is something that happens both physically and mentally, and too much of it will start to take over multiple aspects of your life. As a teen, you are likely dealing with stress related to school, your social life, and your future as a whole. Trying to figure out what college or career path to choose is a lot—and on top of that, keeping up with friends and peers can make things even harder!

Untangle your feelings and stay calm and collected through the practice of labeling emotions! The chart below presents a way for you to examine a feeling and make better sense of it so you can then act accordingly. The first chart is filled out for you as an example:

Basic Emotion	Physical Feelings	Detailed Emotions
Anger	<ul><li>feeling hot/sweating</li><li>tense muscles</li><li>headache</li><li>jaw clenching</li></ul>	<ul><li>rage</li><li>frustration</li><li>resentment</li><li>annoyance</li></ul>
Sadness	<ul><li>feeling tired</li><li>nausea</li><li>body aches</li></ul>	<ul><li>loneliness</li><li>disappointed</li><li>helpless</li></ul>
Joy	<ul><li>butterflies in stomach</li><li>smiling and laughing more</li></ul>	<ul><li>excitement</li><li>satisfaction</li><li>surprise</li></ul>
Fear	<ul><li>biting nails</li><li>restlessness/can't sit still</li><li>uneasiness</li></ul>	<ul><li>panicked</li><li>apprehensive</li><li>worried</li></ul>

As you can see, many emotional branches stem from our main emotions. By putting a more detailed label on what we're feeling, it becomes easier to shine a light on all the ways your mood is impacting you, your environment, or your actions.

In addition, remember to label good emotions just as often as you do the bad. This makes emotional management a more natural habit in your day-to-day life.

Below is an empty template for you to fill out on your own:

Basic Emotion	Physical Feelings	Detailed Emotions

How Can I Recognize What I'm Feeling?

Using the right words can help you make better sense of what you're feeling. Now let's take it a step further and put those emotions and words into full sentences.

One way to get better at understanding your emotions is the use of "I feel" statements. These involve taking responsibility for your emotions, helping you communicate them to others or make more sense of them on your own.

If you know how to keep your cool and stay on top of your emotions, then you ensure your emotions don't get the best of you.

Next, are some practice statements to get you started in the right direction. These feelings-focused statements have some blank spaces for you to fill in with your own emotions or other stressors. Get creative and express yourself by filling these out directly or writing them down in your accompanying notebook:

- I feel _____ when I have a big test coming up.
- _____ makes me feel angry.
- I feel _____ when I have to _____.
- One emotion I don't enjoy feeling is _____.
- Someone who makes me feel _____ is _____.
- One surefire way to make me feel upset is by _____.
- I love _____ because it makes me feel _____.
- When I have to finish a big project, I feel _____.
- When I play a game in gym class, it makes me feel _____.
- I really enjoy _____ with my friends because it makes me feel _____.
- When I'm at home, I feel _____. When I'm at school, I feel _____.
- If I have to do a presentation in class, I usually feel _____.
- I feel _____ when my friends _____.
- When other kids in class _____, it makes me feel _____.
- An activity that always makes me _____ is _____.
- If I didn't have _____, I would feel bad.
- If I didn't have _____, I would feel better.
- The worst I ever felt was _____.
- The best I ever felt was _____.
- I find myself feeling really frustrated when _____.
- _____ always makes me feel agitated.
- I feel the most excited when _____.
- _____ is someone who always seems to feel _____.
- If I get a good grade, I feel _____.

- When I have a lot of homework to do, it makes me feel _____.

- When I start thinking about my future, I feel _____.

- On most days, I feel _____.

- One thing I can do to make myself feel better is _____.

- I haven't felt _____ in a long time.

- The last time I felt _____ was _____.

Why Do I Feel Stressed?

The feelings that our stressors can bring on are often much harder to manage than the actual trigger itself. Research shows that talking about your problem, especially with a friend or loved one, can help reduce negative emotions (Dreher, 2019).

The chart below is a template to help you break your problems down. Once you express how you're feeling, you'll find that you already feel slightly better, making it easier solve problems and get stuff done.

After, you can share this with someone (if you'd like) to help you feel even better and take your emotional expression to the next step. The first chart is filled out with a guide to help you make the most of this activity, with examples included:

My Problem:	*What is the main issue?* What is the problem, conflict, or major stressor that has been taking up your mental energy? List a core problem that you've been struggling with in this box. Examples include: • struggling to maintain good grades • a friend you keep fighting with • hoping you get the spot you are trying out for on your chosen sports team
Feelings:	*What are the mental and physical feelings and emotions attached?* Use the previous emotional labeling activity chart to help you identify some of the effects of this problem. Are you feeling sick with worry? Are you struggling with headaches from stress? Examples of feelings include: • feeling scared about upcoming test results, and struggling to maintain focus because of this • feeling jealous and mad about a group of friends that have been excluding you • feeling nervous and nauseated about upcoming tryouts
My Fear:	*What is the worst-case scenario?* What about this situation causes stress, worry, or panic? What bad thing could happen if your problem takes a turn for the worse? This box can help you label and identify what you are afraid of, helping you see why you might be feeling so stressed. After you write down your fear, you will see that the chances of this happening are a lot less likely than they might initially seem. Examples include: • failing a test • losing a friend

	• not making the team
Help and Support:	*Who can help me with this problem?* Is there a parent, friend, or teacher that can help you get through this issue? Though you might feel alone at times of high stress, there are usually many more systems of support than you realize. Examples include: • a parent who can help pay for a tutor • a sibling who can give advice on managing friendships • a classmate who can help you practice your sport of choice
My Actions:	*What actions can I take to get what I want?* After working through this chart, the last box can be used to help you be more mindful of what actions and realistic steps can be taken so you can overcome this issue once and for all. Examples include: • setting aside an hour a day to study • asking a friend to hang out and talk about why you've been fighting • spending more time practicing and watching other players to help you improve at your sport of choice

Below are some empty templates you can use for various problems you've been struggling with:

My Problem:	
Feelings:	
My Fear:	
Help and Support:	
My Actions:	

My Problem:	
Feelings:	
My Fear:	
Help and Support:	

My Actions:	

My Problem:	
Feelings:	
My Fear:	
Help and Support:	
My Actions:	

My Journal

Research shows that journaling is a great way to improve emotional management and reduce stress (Baran, 2020). Throughout this workbook, you'll find a journal section at the end of each chapter to help you reinforce the different things learned throughout the activities. Use an accompanying notebook to write your responses, or keep a digital journal if you'd prefer typing over writing. Answer these questions in a few sentences or a few pages—the length is up to you! There is no requirement or set of rules for answering each question. They serve as a reflective starting point from which you can branch off in whichever way feels comfortable.

1. What is a feeling you struggle with the most?

2. What is a feeling you often experience that you wish would go away?

3. What is a feeling you enjoy having that you often try to emulate?

4. Think of someone in your life who seems to feel good and be happy often. What do you think contributes to their mood? Now think of someone who seems to feel sad or upset often. Do you think something is going on in their life that might make them feel this way?

5. When was the last time you were able to identify an emotion you were having? What was it, and how did you respond to that feeling?

6. What are your top three stressors?

7. Is it easy for you to identify and share your emotions with other people? Do you feel comfortable sharing the things on your mind?

8. If you could make one problem go away in your life, what would it be and why?

9. When was the last time you acted on your emotions? Are you happy about this, or do you have feelings of regret? What happened after?

10. What are five emotions you've felt in the last three days, and what situation was associated with each emotion?

****

Chapter 2:
Understanding the Power of Self-Care and Creating Productive Routines

What's the last new skill you learned? Maybe you learned how to ride a skateboard or you recently started a new video game.

Chances are, you weren't that great at first. Very few people excel at a skill the first time! But with time and practice, you can grow your skills and talents and become better.

Now, we have to apply this philosophy to our mental health! With time and practice, you can make positive changes in your life that will last a lifetime!

Did You Know?
• Using consistent mindfulness-based techniques helps decrease anxiety and overthinking in adolescents (Abarkar, 2023).
• Self-care is proven to increase self-confidence, productivity, and happiness while reducing the risk of stroke, cancer, and heart disease ("How and Why," 2022).
• Some fast food meals can have more calories in one serving than the calories you need for an entire day ("Take Charge," n.d.).

Self-care is often associated with spa trips or other indulgences. While these can certainly be acts of self-care, the true meaning of nurturing yourself involves ensuring your basic needs are met.

For example, eating a tasty fast food meal can be seen as a form of self-care because we all deserve a treat from time to time. However, ignoring your health and eating fast food daily isn't quite the same. Instead, ensuring your meals are balanced and filled with vitamins and minerals shows that you care for your health and nutrition in the best way possible!

As a teen, your parents or guardians are still responsible for many aspects of your health. For example, they might be your cooking meals or scheduling your doctor's appointments. However, you can still take charge of your mind and body and boost self-care through the use of mindfulness, helping to set yourself up for a future of health and longevity.

My Habits

A habit is something that you do repeatedly. They aren't necessarily good or bad, but instead a way to identify some of the little patterns in our behavior. For example, some good habits include exercising and cleaning consistently. Some bad habits might include leaving messes throughout your home or spending excessive time on social media.

Below are some worksheets to fill out that will help you identify your habits and then transform them into something better for you! There's no right or wrong way to fill these sheets out. By becoming more mindful of how you're spending your time, you can see where bad habits might be causing you to struggle, and where there is room for improvement.

Time Habits

Below is a chart with poor time habits. In the empty square next to each, put a check mark if you've done this before. When you're done, go back through and highlight any that you have done as recently as this week.

	Showed up late to school or work.		Overslept in the morning.
	Procrastinated on a project.		Stayed up too late.
	Forgot about a project's due date.		Rushed through a project.
	Turned something in late.		Skipped studying and failed a test.

Now fill out the chart below with better time habits, following the same rules as above.

	Arrived to work or school early.		Woke up early to study or exercise.
	Finished a project on time.		Went to bed early.
	Followed a study schedule.		Spent adequate time on a project.
	Submitted something early.		Dedicated time to chores.

Take a moment to reflect on both tables. How do they compare? Do you find that you relate more to the box with good time-management habits or the one with poor habits?

Time management is a tricky skill to master, but with practice, you can improve the way you schedule your day-to-day life. If you're mindful in the moment, it becomes easier to stay on top of your routine for a more productive schedule.

Spending Habits

Many companies us advertisements specifically to target teens because they know that you'll be spending your allowances and part-time job income on tasty snacks and treats. Shoppers under 18 don't have to worry about as many bills as adults. Many still live with their parents or guardians, meaning they might have access to more disposable income—any money that is left over after all bills and other costs are paid.

If you're not mindful of spending, you might discover you make impulsive decisions. Have you ever spent money on a clothing item or snack and regretted it later in the day? Can you remember a time you spent birthday money or your allowance on something you wish you hadn't?

Developing better spending habits is important for making smart decisions with your money. Below is a chart of different things on which you can spend any money you receive. List each in chronological order from one to eight, with one being the most important and eight being the least important:

	Food and snacks		Savings account
	Movie or concert tickets		College tuition
	Shoes and clothing		Gas or car expenses
	Hobbies or collectibles		Books and school supplies

Now, consider some goals you have for the future. Do your spending habits align with these goals? For example, if you want to move out of state and attend a specific university to earn a degree, you might struggle to achieve this if your top spending priority is clothes or shoes. Mindful spending will help you focus on the things that are the most important to you so you can spend less on things that don't match up with what you want for your future.

Study Habits

Studying is a crucial part of academic success. You don't have to be at the top of your class, but getting good grades to earn a high school diploma will open up more opportunities for you in the future.

Use the chart below to reflect on some of your academic habits. To make improvements, you have to first identify what might be holding you back:

The things I'm good at in school are...	The things I struggle with in school are...

When you identify your strengths, it's easier to find a solution to deal with your weaknesses. Some people might do great with mathematics while others do best in literature. Some students love working in groups in the classroom, while others do their best learning at home on their own. Either way, you can find what works for you to succeed academically when you are more mindful about your school habits.

Building a Goal

Take a moment to reflect on some of the things you've learned about yourself in the past three habit-related activities. Between time management, spending habits, and your study skills, what area do you do best in? What area do you want to do better in?

A goal is a dream, desire, or wish you have for the future. To reach your goal, you have to know what steps to take to get there. These small steps are called objectives. Goals can have a couple of objectives, or there can be many involved. For example, someone wanting to compete in the Olympics as a swimmer will have to start small, with objectives like finding a trainer or joining their school's team. Goals can be smaller and shorter too, like wanting to earn a B or higher on a test. The objectives involved in this might simply be to read a book or make notecards.

Let's start the process of goal-setting now! Focus on having the process become the goal. For example, you would write down a goal of exercising three days a week rather than saying you want to lose 10 pounds in two months. You might try reading 20 pages a day rather than studying for a test. Try this method when labeling goals.

Below, write down your top five goals, both big and small:

1. _____
2. _____
3. _____
4. _____
5. _____

Next, take each goal and break it down into at least five different steps using the template below. Get as detailed as possible with these steps to help you make it easier to achieve these objectives and find success.

My Goal: _____

Step One	
Step Two	
Step Three	
Step Four	
Step Five	

My Goal: _____

Step One	
Step Two	
Step Three	
Step Four	
Step Five	

My Goal: _____

Step One	
Step Two	
Step Three	
Step Four	
Step Five	

My Goal: _____

Step One	
Step Two	
Step Three	
Step Four	
Step Five	

My Goal: _____

Step One	
Step Two	
Step Three	
Step Four	
Step Five	

My Routines

Next up is a seven-day schedule to help you track your routines and notice how you spend your time. This can help you feel more organized so that it becomes easier to keep up with extracurricular activities and stay on top of studying. Before you create better habits, it can be helpful to identify the ones you are currently struggling with.

Instructions

Consistent routines are important for your health. If you can identify the things you do that might harm your health, it becomes easier to break bad habits and build better ones.

Below are two templates for you to fill out that will help you become more mindful of how you spend your time.

Part One: The first step is to track your time for one week to see how you spend your days.

- Wake Time: Note when you wake up.

- Activities: This column will include any chores, hobbies, or studying you participated in.

- Emotions: Use specific words to identify how you feel throughout the day.

- Sleep Time: Note when you go to bed.

Part Two: The second step is to fill out the Daily Planner template to help you create a more productive routine. Use your goals from the last activity and develop a day-to-day process that works for your needs.

- Today's Goal: Think of a goal you have for the day. A daily goal might be one of the objectives listed in the previous activity.

- Checklist: Create a list of the tasks involved in reaching this goal.

- Schedule: Jot down a basic schedule of your day with estimated starting and end times for the various tasks in your day.

- Today's High: Label the best thing that happened that day.

- Today's Low: Identify the worst part of your day or a time you struggled.

Daily Tracker

Day	Wake Time	Activities	Emotions	Sleep Time
Monday				
Tuesday				
Wednesday				
Thursday				
Friday				
Saturday				
Sunday				

Evaluating Your Results

Once you've finished filling out the daily tracker, you can look at the boxes and start to notice patterns. For example, on the days when you felt the most negative emotions, it might've been due to waking up late or a specific activity you did that day. You can also gain a fresh perspective on how you prioritize and manage your time, helping you become more mindful of how you spend each day.

Daily Planner

Today's Goal	
Checklist	
Schedule	
Today's High	

Today's Low

My Health

The last section will help guide you through your health.

Right now, you're experiencing a time of major changes! For this reason, your body needs the right amount of exercise, nutrition, sleep, and stress management to help you grow in the best way possible!

There are four parts to nurture to maintain good health, and these can be referred to as the four corners of health:

- mental health
- sleep
- physical
- nutritional

Together, these four elements combine to create a perfect box that upholds your health. Knowing how to optimize these four corners can be tricky, however. Below is a reference box that provides you with different health standards to follow as a teen. Mental health is harder to measure, and the less stress endured, the better. That's why mindfulness is so important to help you maintain strong mental health. Aside from mental health, the other three corners have some more specific requirements to ensure you are maintaining your health. These are based on the Centers for Disease Control and Prevention standards:

Sleep	Food	Exercise
Amount of daily sleep suggested: - 6-12 years: 9-12 hours - 13-18 years: 8-10 hours The more consistent and regulated your sleep schedule is, the more likely you are to have high-quality sleep. Napping is also a way to supplement your sleep to reach the recommended hours. (Just make sure it's early in the day to avoid disrupting your sleep before bed).	Foods to eat more of: - fruits and vegetables such as leafy greens and antioxidant-rich berries - whole grains such as whole wheat bread, oatmeal, and brown rice - protein-rich foods such as fish, chicken, and tofu - low-fat dairy products such as cottage cheese and yogurt	The recommended amount of daily physical activity for those ages 6-17: - 60 minutes of a combination of aerobic, muscle-strengthening, and bone-strengthening exercises. Examples include: - biking - running - swimming - lifting weights

Next, let's do a self-assessment so you can test how well you are currently maintaining the four corners of your health. This isn't to determine whether you are healthy—only a licensed medical professional can determine this for you in person through various exams and tests. However, you can raise your mindfulness of how well you are taking care of yourself by reflecting on the way you feel about your health. For each section, rate the statement between one and five using this scale:

1. I completely disagree with this statement and don't relate to it at all.

2. I mostly disagree with this statement but can relate on a rare occasion.

3. I sometimes disagree with this and sometimes agree with this statement.

4. I mostly agree with this statement but can't fully relate.

5. I completely agree with this statement and relate to what is said.

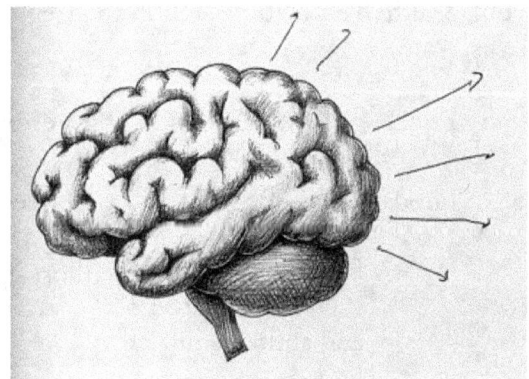

Mental Health

Rating	Statement
	I rarely experience stress or anxiety.
	I feel confident in who I am and I'm not afraid to be myself.
	I feel supported and validated by the people around me.
	When something stressful happens, I can handle it with ease.
	I practice mindfulness and awareness frequently.

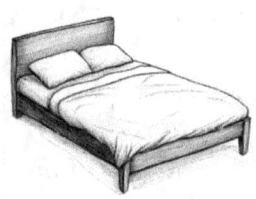

Sleep Health

Rating	Statement
	I make sure to go to bed at a good time every night.
	I give myself plenty of time to get ready and wake up in the morning.
	I follow a consistent sleep routine.
	I get at least eight hours of sleep every night.
	It's important for me to get a good night's sleep.

Physical Health

Rating	Statement
	I make sure to dedicate part of my day to physical activity.

	I feel confident in my physical strength.
	It's easy for me to be physically active.
	I'm comfortable with athletics.
	I fully understand the importance of physical movement.

Nutritional Health

Rating	Statement
	I pay attention to how fast I eat.
	I try to listen to my body and don't eat too much when I feel full.
	It's easy for me to control portions and pick nutritious foods.
	I understand the importance of eating nutritious foods.
	I enjoy learning about nutritional health and like studying healthy foods.

Your Results

Now, add up your responses to get your total score. Depending on what score you get, you can learn a few different things about how to be more mindful with your mind and body:

- **20-49**: You might be struggling to make important decisions for your health, and self-care is likely hard for you to participate in. If this is the case, you might consider reaching out to a parent, teacher, doctor, or guidance counselor to help you build some better habits.

- **50-69**: You likely practice a small form of self-care, but there are areas where you could use some improvement. If this is the score you got, a good next step to take is to do some research on your health so you can boost your knowledge in the area that is lacking.

- **70-89**: If you received this score, chances are you are taking some good steps to maintain your health! Now, take it to the next level and create a stronger routine and better habits around sleep, nutrition, and physical health.

- **90-100**: If this is your score, you are doing many of the right things to stay mindful of your health and body. But don't stop there! Keep maintaining good habits and routines so you can ensure you are getting the best care possible.

If you find that one area scores particularly low, it's also important to take the right steps to find more balance among the four corners.

My Journal

The best person to take care of you is you! By staying mindful of your health and focusing on building solid routines, you will be sure to set yourself up for success.

- How has your relationship with your health changed over the years?
- Who helps you with self-care?
- What is one thing you wish you could change about your routine?
- What is the highlight of most of your days?

- How often do you feel mindful throughout the day?

- Are you more mindful of yourself or focused on others? What led you to this answer?

- Describe your ideal schedule, including all of the things you'd want to get done in a day. How different does this look from the current schedule you have, and what, if anything, can you do to make improvements?

- Do you enjoy the elements of self-care, or do they feel like more of a chore?

- Which of the four corners of health do you struggle with the most? Do you notice any ways that this impacts the other three corners?

- What is your proudest achievement? What habits did it take to help you accomplish this?

****

Chapter 3:
Getting Organized for Present and Future Success

Does your mind ever feel like an overstuffed, chaotic, messy closet? You're not alone! As a teen, all of these feelings, thoughts, and emotions can make your mindset feel messy. Not only does mindfulness calm the chaos—it unlocks new parts of your brain to have more control over the decisions and choices you make!

> **Did You Know?**
>
> - The last part of the brain to develop is the prefrontal cortex, which is responsible for decision-making and planning ("The Teen Brain," n.d.).
>
> - Ninety-five percent of the brain structure is developed by five or six years old, but that structure changes over time due to experiences we live through and decisions we make (Spinks, n.d.).
>
> - Over half of high school students are optimistic about their future (Bryant, 2022).

A mind filled with fear, anger, and other difficult emotions can make it difficult to focus on the things that require our attention.

For example, feeling scared about a test you have at the end of the day might consume your mind, eating away at every last thought. This means you'll be missing out on important lessons in other classes. Alternatively, if you find yourself fighting with a friend, that might make it hard to enjoy spending time with your family at at home.

Little things can creep into your mind where they can grow bigger, scarier, and harder to handle. By practicing mindfulness, you can take these challenging emotions and learn to sit through them, reducing their distraction. By lowering the control they have over your mindset, you will have an easier time staying calm and focused through the stress so you can make the best decisions possible, reducing conflict and anxiety.

Daily Mindfulness

Below is a reference box that provides ideas for activities to help you practice daily mindfulness in an easy, exciting, and realistic way. These are quick activities that can be done in under five minutes so you can add more acts of mindfulness to your routine. Mindfulness doesn't have to be a strenuous process!

They are also great things to practice when you are feeling worried about something in the future or can't seem to let go of something in the past.

Breathwork	Start by counting from one to five. Go slow, ensuring you leave about a second-long pause in between each number. Once you find a steady pace, breathe in for five seconds, then breathe out for five seconds. Notice how you feel after. What changed?
Ice Cube Trick	Grab an ice cube and hold it as it melts. Notice the way it feels in your hand and watch as it changes shape.
Pocket Mindfulness	Find a small notebook that you can keep in your pocket. When you are feeling anxious, jot down your anxious thoughts. Notice how you feel after. Are you less tense or anxious?
Color Identification	Identify everything in the room that is a specific color. Notice how this changes your focus so you can redirect your

	thoughts.
Find 10 Things	Look around the room to see if there are multiples of anything. If so, count at least ten. Notice how your mind feels after you count.
Flat Feet, Flat Hands	Change whatever position you are in to make your feet and your hands completely flat, releasing tension in the process. Notice how both your mind and body feel after this practice.
Funny Face	Make the funniest face you can! Notice how a simple change to your expression can impact your mood, and even the way your body feels.
Opposite Hand	Use the pointer finger on your non-dominant hand to write your name on your leg or arm. Notice the way your attention shifts.
Object Trace	Find a small object that you can grab. Trace the shape of it using your finger. Notice the way it feels in your hands.
Smile	Look around and smile as big as you can. Notice how your body feels or if your mood changes.

Another type of important mindfulness practice is mindfulness meditation. One kind of meditation to try is a body scan. Using the same breathwork technique from the chart above, start to regulate your breathing. Find a comfortable pace and start to clear your mind.

As you do this, focus on each part of your body, starting at the top and slowly scanning down. Concentrate on your head, lingering there for a moment as you bring a feeling of awareness to each part.

Move down to your shoulders, arms, and chest. Let out all of the tension, and keep focusing on letting your mind become more and more relaxed. Repeat the process as you travel down to your stomach, hips, thighs, and knees. Breathe as you linger on your knees and calves, ankles, and feet.

Your body will become more and more relaxed with each area you pass. Once you reach your feet, start scanning back up. Repeat this scan as needed until you feel relaxed and at peace. This is a great practice to do before school, after you're done for the day, and before bed at night.

Following a Budget

This activity involves creating a budget so you can build mindfulness around how you spend and save money. Mindless spending can lead to an endless pool of stressful situations. While you might not have a ton of financial responsibilities right now, it's never too early to develop a mindful relationship with spending!

A basic budget has two main parts:
- Income: Income refers to any source of money. This might include an allowance or money you make from working.

- Expenses: This includes any bills or savings account deposits. Bills involve things like paying for electricity and water for your home. Savings accounts are methods of storing finances for later use. You likely don't have bills to pay, but you might have small expenses, like streaming service subscriptions, or having gas and spending money for hanging out with friends.

Below is a blank template for you to use to build a budget. This way, you can start to track some of the ways you spend, making you more mindful of your money habits.

Budget Template

Income	Amount	Expense	Amount

Teen Accountability

What does accountability mean to you? Accountability refers to our ability to account for the things we've done. In simple terms, it's your way of owning up to what mistakes or decisions you've made, and doing something to make up for that in the future.

Remember as a kid when your parents would tell you to say sorry? You'd say sorry, but then the dreadful question came: "Sorry for what?". When we clarified what we were sorry for, that was us taking accountability. Saying a simple word like "sorry" is one thing, but owning up to the stuff you actually did is the important part.

Accountability is an important thing to have because it's how we learn from mistakes and move on to become a better version of ourselves. It's not always easy to admit we're wrong because we might be afraid of looking dumb or feeling embarrassed. However, by saying we're sorry and moving on, we can learn from the experience so it doesn't happen again, rather than ignoring the problem and having it happen again later.

Accountability is something shared with others, but it's also something we can show ourselves. For example, if you fail a test, holding yourself accountable would mean admitting you could have studied more. If you blame your sibling for distracting you or the teacher for making the test too hard, you fail to take accountability and might not put as much effort into studying in the future.

When it comes to mindfulness, accountability is important because it shows we are practicing self-awareness. Use the chart below to help you get started in the process of self-accountability. If you're still struggling to understand accountability, there is an example filled out after the template:

A time I regret my words or actions was... **After this happened, I...**	
A time I was wrong was when... **I responded to this by...**	
A time I was wrong but didn't admit it right away was when... **What resulted was...**	

These guided exercises will help you boost self-awareness so you can learn to be more mindful of the way you interact with others. Accountability is important so we can become aware of how our words or actions not only affect what happens to us but also how we make an impact on other people. Below is an example chart filled out for you to help you understand what it looks like to be mindful.

A time I regret my words or actions was...	*when I told my friend their favorite band was lame.*
After this happened, I...	*apologized and said I was being too judgemental.*
A time I was wrong was when...	*I was mean to my siblings during dinner the other night.*
I responded to this by...	*spending time playing a game with them the next day and apologizing for what I said.*
A time I was wrong but didn't admit it right away was when...	*I got really mad and slammed the locker room door after my team lost.*
What resulted was...	*I got in trouble for bad sportsmanship with my coach and couldn't play the next game.*

My Journal

Your mindfulness skills will grow when you make an effort to practice awareness every day. This will help you focus on improving your skills rather than getting lost in self-doubt or second-guessing your abilities. If you stay focused and keep your mind free from stressful thoughts, you'll find that it becomes easier to boost motivation and productivity. Below are some prompts to help you become even more mindful in the present and improve your organizational skills:

- What does it mean to you to be responsible?

- How can you use accountability skills to stay more organized with your responsibilities?

- Take a moment to list all of your responsibilities. Out of these, which is the most important? Why is it important for you to uphold these responsibilities?

- Who is the most responsible person you know? Why do you think they are good at fulfilling their obligations?

- What is your favorite method of mindfulness?

- Can you recall a time when you were disorganized? What were the consequences, if any?

- Think of a time when you realized you were being irresponsible, such as procrastinating when you knew you should be studying. Did you take action to fix this?

- How would you describe your knowledge of money?

- How long does it take you to feel like you are being mindful when practicing mindfulness?

- What has been the most valuable lesson you've learned so far in the readings?

****

Chapter 4:
Fostering Self-Love and Boosting Empowerment With Confidence

Have you ever seen a piece of clothing on a mannequin or a model on an online store and thought they looked great? But then you buy the clothing for yourself, only to think it looks terrible?

Often, we are much harder on ourselves than we are on other people. It's easy to pick out all your flaws because you see yourself every day! However, other people don't notice the same things you do, so it's time to stop being so hard on yourself and practice self-love.

> **Did You Know?**
>
> - As much as 85% of the global population has low self-esteem (Guttman, 2019).
> - Only 55% of teenage girls feel confident (Peetz, 2023).
> - Teens with high self-esteem are proven to be more successful later in life in terms of school, work, health, and relationships (Blouin, 2022).

Life can be stressful at times, but it can also be filled with fun and amazing adventures! However, it's hard to feel this way when you're lacking confidence in yourself.

Sometimes when we think about confidence, an image of a self-absorbed person might come to mind, but that's not the case! Confidence is important to help boost your self-esteem. When you are confident, you can stay more present in the moment. You become less focused on what others might think or potential failures.

That's not to say that those who are confident are without fear! Instead, confident people can know they are capable of achieving great things and are willing to take the risks needed to get what they want.

My Own Best Friend

We can be very hard on ourselves. Sometimes, the biggest bully we face is the voice in our own head. And it's hard to re-tune that voice if you aren't aware of just how destructive it is on your life. Self-compassion is proven to lead to higher levels of success (Martin, 2023). Learning how to become your own best friend is a great way to be more mindful of the relationship you have with yourself.

These next few exercises will serve to help you strengthen your confidence and fine-tune your inner voice.

Letter Through Time

1. Think back to a part of your childhood that was somewhat challenging. Whether this was a difficult experience or you went through something tough, identify what the obstacle was.

2. Now, write a letter to who you were at this time. Use language that you would understand if you were really young. Talk about life now, and include anything you might want to say to this version of yourself.

3. Tell yourself what ended up happening, and use encouraging language to remind yourself that you made it through. Let your mind flow freely and write down anything else that comes to mind. When we look back on younger versions of ourselves, we can become more forgiving. We didn't know better back then! By learning how to be compassionate and nurturing to yourself, you make it easier to boost confidence.

Thank You Note

1. Think back to a time when you made a mistake.

2. Now, get creative and find a way to thank yourself for this. For example, if you got in trouble and received detention in junior high, you might feel regretful because of your actions. However, if you can learn to forgive yourself, it becomes easier to move on. You might even thank yourself for this mistake because you ended up meeting your best friend in detention!

3. Acknowledge what you did wrong, and remember that it's important to stay accountable. If we can learn how to forgive and find something positive in the negative, it's easier to manage feelings of guilt or shame.

Good Friend, Bad Friend

Use the chart below to fill out what it means to be a good friend versus a bad friend. A few examples are provided to get you started:

Good Friend	Bad Friend
• Is nice and supportive	• Says mean things and name-calls
• Shares fun experiences with others	• Tries to control other people
•	•
•	•
•	•
•	•
•	•
•	•
•	•

Once you've filled out the chart, take a moment to consider if you are a good friend to yourself. We tend to be nice to others without showing ourselves the same compassion.

Identify some things you said to yourself in the past that were harsh. Would you say these things to another friend? Chances are, you wouldn't! But for some reason, we don't think twice when we say mean things to ourselves.

Reflect on how you can start to speak to yourself in a kinder way. By doing this, you can help yourself become a better and more supportive friend in the process.

The Power of Affirmations

Have you heard of affirmations before? It might sound like a big word, but really, it's a simple concept! An affirmation is a simple statement, and usually one that states a truth. Affirmations come in the form of different things we say to ourselves. Examples of common affirmations include:

- I can do this.
- I hate waking up.
- I am a student.

As you can see, these simple phrases are a mix of positive, neutral, and negative. An affirmation is neither good nor bad, but rather a tool we can use to help us change our mindset. Follow the steps below to use affirmations:

1. The first step in using affirmations is to identify the negative things you say to yourself. These are often limiting beliefs and harsh things that simply aren't true.

2. Next, turn these negative affirmations into a more neutral statement. Neutral means that it isn't mean or nice, just something that is considered somewhere in the middle.

3. Lastly, turn these neutral statements into positive and uplifting ones. When you start to replace negative affirmations with positive ones, you will find that your confidence multiplies.

Below are some examples of affirmations to help you identify and change the way you talk to yourself.

Negative Affirmations

- I am not good enough.
- I can't do this.
- Everything is terrible.
- I'll never get what I want.
- I'm such a failure.
- No one likes me.
- Everyone is more talented than me.
- I'm not good at anything.
- School is the worst.
- Something is always going wrong.

Neutral Statements

- I have strengths and weaknesses.
- Some tasks are more challenging than others.
- Life is filled with ups and downs.
- I have to work hard to get what I want.
- I'm not perfect, but I'm still successful.
- I have friends and family members in my life.
- Everyone has different skill levels.

- I have some things I can improve on.
- School can be challenging.
- Unexpected things can happen but things usually end up okay.

Positive Affirmations

- I am powerful and talented.
- I am brave enough to take on any task.
- Life is an amazing journey!
- I am dedicated and passionate.
- I have so many accomplishments to be proud of.
- Many people love me.
- There are many things I'm good at.
- I am a fast learner and a dedicated student.
- I am smart and educated.
- I am prepared for anything.

Bird's-Eye View

The last activity involves a chart to help you gain a third-person perspective on your life or situation. A third-person perspective helps to induce more reflective and objective thinking, both things that help reduce overthinking and improve mindfulness.

Objective thinking means not really having an opinion on something. Opinions can come across as judgmental, and when we feel like we are being judged, it can make us feel insecure and hurt our self-esteem. To be more mindful of the objective truth of your life, you can practice using this third-person exercise to remove some of the judgments you've placed on yourself.

The chart involves rows including:

- **One-Sentence Summary**: This is a quick description of your situation and a little bit about who you are.

- **Setting and Time Period**: This is for the location and year.

- **Characters**: This includes anyone who is a major character in your life, like a parent, friend, or even pet!

- **Conflict**: This box is for any major conflicts and struggles you've been experiencing.

- **Themes**: Lastly is the theme. This might include things like education, athletics, nature, or art. What main themes exist in your life?

Get creative with this and think outside of the box when telling your story!

My Story

One-Sentence Summary	
Setting	
Time Period	

Characters	
Conflict	
Themes	

Third Person

My Journal

Learning to love yourself isn't an easy process and is something many adults continue to struggle with well into later years! However, by practicing self-love at an early age, you will set yourself up for future empowerment and long-lasting confidence. Below are some reflection questions and journal prompts to help you stay more mindful, allowing for more room to boost your self-esteem:

- What do you love most about yourself?

- What do you wish you could change about yourself?

- Who is someone you believe is confident? What about them shows they have a high level of self-esteem?

- When was the last time you felt truly confident? How did this change your behavior?

- Can you recall a time that someone hurt your self-esteem? What did they say or do to cause this?

- Is there something you can do that instantly boosts your confidence?

- Rumination is the act of repeatedly going through past experiences and feeling anxious about them. For example, someone might ruminate over an embarrassing thing they said or did. Do you find yourself struggling with rumination? When was the last time you ruminated?

- Has mindfulness helped boost your confidence so far? If not, how do you think you can elicit confidence through mindfulness?

- On a scale of 1-10, how much importance do you place on the opinions others have of you?

- Who is your role model? What about them do you want to emulate in yourself?

****

Chapter 5:
Navigating Relationships and Managing Your Social Life

Mindfulness can help improve your relationships and strengthen your connections for a healthier social life.

> **Did You Know?**
>
> - Those with larger social networks tend to have higher self-esteem (Masselink, 2017).
>
> - Eighty-three percent of teens who use social media state they feel more connected to their friends because of their social media use (Lenhart, 2015).
>
> - Studies show that people are likely to follow the beliefs of a crowd and conform even when they actively disagree with the majority opinion (Cherry, 2023).

School is filled with many challenges—especially social ones. It's easy to feel insecure and like others are judging you, especially when you have to do something challenging like play a sport or perform in a school play. Using some of these communication and mindfulness tips will help you maintain a strong social circle so you always have a system of support.

Surviving School

This activity will help you build a mindfulness toolkit so you will always have something on hand to help you feel grounded and present, no matter what you run into.

Mindfulness Toolkit Guidelines

Suggested Object	Examples
Trinket	- pebble - coin - bottle cap *Rub this between your thumb and pointer finger when you are feeling anxious and need to be grounded in the present.
Book or Notebook	- a book of poems - a book of short stories - a notebook for jotting down feelings
Small Activity	- a small piece of wood and a carving tool - a piece of clay to mold - a crochet needle and some yarn
Picture	- a picture of someone you love - a picture of a place where you feel safe - a picture of something you want in the future
Fidget Toy	- something soft and squishy to play with when feeling overwhelmed with thoughts - a small toy you can play with

	• a piece of velcro to fidget with

Once you've gathered your items, creating something that can hold your mindfulness resources is the next important step. This way, you will always know exactly where to go when you're feeling stressed and overwhelmed. Consider decorating an old shoe box or using a small bag to hold your mindfulness objects.

Foundational Friendships

Positive peer influence is proven to improve a teen's health, so it's crucial to raise mindfulness about your friendships and other relationships (Neff, 2023).

This section includes an informational table to help you identify healthy versus unhealthy friendships. One column includes things you'll see with healthy bonds, and the other has red flags. You can return to this reference box when assessing relationships to determine if the bonds you're experiencing are hurtful or harmful:

Red Flag	Healthy Bond
The other person makes you feel uncomfortable or scared to speak up.	You have fun with the other person and laugh often.
The other person tries to isolate you from others.	You can spend time with other people and have fun in groups.
The other person uses things against you,	You can open up and feel comfortable in

makes threats, and calls you names.	front of the other person.
The other person prevents you from doing the things you want.	You feel supported and free in the relationship.
The other person physically harms you.	You feel safe and respected by the other person.

Communication Tips

Below is a chart you can reference to help you better communicate.

Sometimes, it's not that you don't know what to say or how you're feeling, but rather, you aren't sure how to express this in the best way possible. We don't want to hurt the feelings of others, and we don't want to cause even more conflict, so navigating the various ways you can express yourself is a challenge. However, with practice, you'll be able to not only share how you feel but do so in a way that makes things even better than they were before.

The first column provides some scenarios you might be struggling with. The second offers example phrases you can use and tweak as needed to cater to your specific situation. Practice these phrases to help you fine tune your voice!

Scenario	Example Phrases
How to ask for help if a relationship has a lot of red flags:	• Can I talk to you about a friend I have? • How can you tell if a friend is a good or bad one?
How to communicate needs effectively:	• I am feeling [insert feeling here], and I think talking about it would help. • Lately, I've been struggling with [insert emotion here] and would love to talk about it with you.
How to say no:	• I appreciate you asking, but I can't. • Not this time, but maybe next time! • I won't be able to do that right now.

How to set a boundary:	• When you do [insert behavior] it makes me feel [insert emotion]. Going forward, I need things to change. • I don't like when you [insert behavior], and for my own mental health, I can't be around you when you do that.

Happy at Home

Mindfulness is something that can be spread among the whole family. These are ideas to keep families closer and make everyone happier in the process! When you feel safe at home, you can be more present in the moment, reducing stress and raising awareness. The following activities are great ways to boost the whole family's mindfulness!

1. **Family Garden:** Start a garden with your family where you can grow herbs, fruits, and vegetables. Take turns caring for the garden, and cook meals together with your harvest!

2. **Family Game Night:** Set aside a weekly game night to play with your family. Make a rule that no phones are allowed, and swap out what games you play to keep things exciting.

3. **Family Movie Club:** Take turns picking out a movie to watch each week. After the movie is over, spend some time talking about what you watched. Just like game night, consider the rule that no phones are allowed!

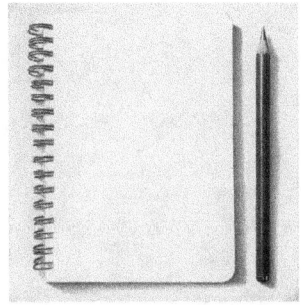

My Journal

Mindfulness will help you manage your thoughts, but beyond that, it will also be helpful in your relationships. You can work through conflict and create even better connections by making a dedication to more mindful living. Below are some final reflection questions and prompts you can use with other people! Ask these questions to friends or family members to start a discussion and create a more productive conversation!

- What goals do you have for the future?

- What is the hardest part about school? What is the best part about school?

- What is the most valuable mindfulness tool you have?

- Do you think your relationships are generally good or generally bad?

- What is the hardest part about communicating with other people?

- Who are you the closest to out of everyone you know?

- Why are friendships important to you?

- What is one goal you have for your relationships with other people?

- How do you think mindfulness could impact the way you interact with others both at school and at home?

- What is one thing you hope to use mindfulness for in the future?

****

BONUS:

21-Day Action Plan

Learning about mindfulness is important, but now it's time to take what we've talked about and apply it to your life!

Over the next 21 days, your challenge is to follow along with this three-week plan. Each week, you'll take the concepts covered in the book and maximize their effect by completing simple daily challenges.

Under the column "Your Thoughts," write down your experiences with the daily challenge. Did you finish it, or did you run into any issues? Did you learn anything? Use a notebook if needed.

After the daily challenges, there is a table to write down your reflections on the week. Discuss anything you learned, realized, or became aware of during your mindful challenge. Discuss successes by listing anything you gained or accomplished. Lastly, create a couple of small goals for yourself to keep in mind for the rest of the week.

Week One: Unlock Your Mind

This first week is all about noticing, feeling, and raising awareness. The first stage of mindfulness involves recognizing where you are now; that way you know what to focus on! Read through Chapters 1 and 2, and do as many activities as possible this first week.

Daily To-Dos

Day	Your Challenge	Your Thoughts
Monday	Identify a feeling you have today. Notice what might have caused it, and what you do as a result of this feeling.	
Tuesday	Set a timer and spend 10 minutes journaling today. Identify how you felt before, during, and after journaling.	
Wednesday	Notice any physical feelings that come along with your emotions today. Evaluate how these impact the rest of your day.	
Thursday	Label a habit you have. Discuss why this habit developed, and whether or not it is good or bad for you.	
Friday	Reflect on your health, both physical and mental. Discuss if you are happy with this, or if you want to make improvements.	
Saturday	Create a goal for your future. Use the template from Chapter 2 to help you break down this goal.	
Sunday	Spend the day filling out your weekly reflections, and be as thorough as possible.	

Weekly Reflections

What I Learned, Realized, or Became Aware Of:	What I Gained or Accomplished:	What I Will Continue to Improve:

Week Two: Amplify Your Power

Now that you know what it means to be truly mindful, let's take it to the next stage. Follow these challenges while you read Chapters 3 and 4, and do as many chapter activities as you can.

Daily To-Dos

Day	Your Challenge	Your Thoughts
Monday	Practice breathwork. Notice how you felt before and after.	
Tuesday	Pick out another type of daily mindfulness, and practice this. Discuss any mental or physical changes you experience.	
Wednesday	Reflect on your money habits, and notice any patterns you see between these habits and your emotional state.	
Thursday	Reflect on your journals from last week, and notice if anything has changed in your thought process.	
Friday	Notice your relationships and how they impact your thoughts and feelings.	

Saturday	Practice affirmations. Discuss your feelings before, during, and after practicing.	
Sunday	Fill in your weekly reflections. Look at this week compared to last week. What has changed?	

Weekly Reflections

What I Learned, Realized, or Became Aware Of:	What I Gained or Accomplished:	What I Will Continue to Improve:

Week Three: Practice, Practice, Practice!

This last week is all about reinforcing what you've learned and weaving it into your daily routines, habits, and thoughts. Finish up reading Chapter 5, and use the rest of the week to go back and finish any worksheets or activities you haven't finished yet.

Daily To-Dos

Day	Your Challenge	Your Thoughts
Monday	Identify what you have learned about yourself most in this process.	
Tuesday	Create your mindfulness toolkit (See Chapter 5 for instructions).	
Wednesday	Reflect on a relationship that makes you feel good about yourself. What qualities in this person help you feel your best?	
Thursday	Identify your strengths and weaknesses with communication. How can you use this knowledge to improve communication in the future?	
Friday	Create a goal you have for the future, and write down what will motivate you to get there.	

Saturday	Finish your weekly reflections, then go back and compare all three weeks. What do you notice?	
Sunday	Spend the day celebrating your success of completing the 21-day challenge!	

Weekly Reflections

What I Learned, Realized, or Became Aware Of:	What I Gained or Accomplished:	What I Will Continue to Improve:

Final Thoughts

In less than a month, you've noticed yourself becoming more mindful by staying consistent with these challenges! Try repeating this activity with a friend to help them become more mindful too!

The key is consistency, so keep practicing and see your mind's full potential! The beauty of mindfulness is that there is no risk, and it's completely safe to try. It might not change your life the first time you practice it, but each moment you dedicate to being mindful will help lead you down the path of greater awareness. Give yourself the gift of powerful knowledge and keep practicing these tips, tricks, and habits!

Conclusion

"Take a moment to acknowledge your efforts, every step counts!"

How has your ability to be mindful changed throughout the readings? Do you feel more mindful than you did when you first started this book? Mindfulness is a practice that you can chip away at over time, making small improvements here and there.

Look for small ways to be more mindful every day. By using these little building blocks over time, you'll create an unbreakable foundation of awareness that will carry with you through life. Think of your mindfulness practice as a single brick in a solid wall. These walls are building a support system for your future so that you always know what steps to take when you're feeling overwhelmed or confronted by unexpected challenges.

Stress and anxiety can be triggered later in life, but mindfulness is the tool that will help serve as a reminder that peace is possible. There's so much to be excited about in the upcoming years. Meeting new people, gaining independence, and heading off to new schools might be some of the things you have to look forward to. However, these big changes and unexpected situations can also bring on plenty of anxiety, so learning how to use grounding techniques will keep you present throughout them all.

Your mind is developing right now, and understanding and navigating the emotions you're struggling with can be complicated. Remember that what you are feeling is normal, and raising awareness of the present moment around you can help with decreasing anxious thoughts and feelings.

As you move through the next few years, remember to follow these tips to foster awareness:

- Be present and notice how the emotional states you're experiencing connect to how your body feels.

- Make sure your basic needs are met and prioritize finding balance in life.

- Notice how the way you interact with others can impact them and how you can improve relationships in the process.

- Remind yourself you are worthy of love and stay grounded to help maintain a healthy level of self-esteem.

- Stay consistent with mindfulness and share these experiences with others for a happy life at school and at home.

Each day is a new opportunity to be mindful. The world and the future are filled with endless opportunities. Explore the possibility and unlock your potential!

If you've enjoyed this workbook, could you please take a moment to leave an Amazon review?

Your feedback helps others find this book and spreads the joy of mindfulness. Share what resonated most with you and how these activities have supported your path to mindfulness. THANK YOU for your help!

It has been a privilege to be your guide in this workbook. May you continue to grow and find joy in your mindfulness journey ahead.

***

Did you enjoy this book? Read the next book in C.J.Kindren's Teen Series:

A Teen's Guide to Quit Ultra-Processed Foods Now
>> https://books2read.com/teen-upf

Your Voice Can Change Lives

Keeping the Mindfulness Movement Growing!

"We rise by lifting others." - Robert Ingersoll

You've made it to the end of our mindfulness journey together! Now that you have these powerful tools to handle stress, manage emotions, and stay balanced, you can help other teens find their path to peace too.

Think about how you felt before starting this book - maybe stressed about school, worried about relationships, overwhelmed by social media, or just looking for ways to feel better. There are so many other teens out there feeling exactly the same way right now.

Your Review Could Help Someone Who Is...

…Struggling to handle school pressure and homework

…Having a hard time with friendships or family relationships

…Feeling overwhelmed by social media and constant connectivity

…Trying to figure out who they are and where they fit in

…Looking for ways to feel more peaceful and balanced

…Dealing with anxiety or stress alone

By sharing your honest thoughts about Find Your Balance on Amazon, you become part of something bigger. Your review could be the reason someone else discovers these life-changing mindfulness techniques! It doesn't have to be long or perfect - just genuine. Share what you found most helpful or what surprised you about mindfulness.

Remember how mindfulness is about awareness and being present? This is your chance to be present for others who need support. Your words could be exactly what another teen needs to hear to take their first step toward better mental health.

Ready to Help Another Teen Find Their Balance?

Simply follow these links to leave your review on your local Amazon marketplace:

Thank you for being part of this mindfulness community. Together, we're creating a more peaceful, balanced world - one teen at a time!

Keep practicing those mindfulness skills, and remember: your voice matters! Whether you're using the companion notebook or creating your own mindfulness journey, every small step counts toward building a more mindful future.

With gratitude and peace, C.J. Kindren

References

Abarkar, Z., Ghasemi, M., Manesh, E.M., Mehdibeygi Sarvestani, M., Moghbeli, N., Rostamipoor, N., Seifi, Z., Ardakani, M.B. (2023). *The effectiveness of adolescent-oriented mindfulness training on academic burnout and social anxiety symptoms in students: experimental research.* NIH. https://www.ncbi.nlm.nih.gov/pmc/articles/PMC10289713/

Beresin, G. (2022, September 23). *Stress in teenagers.* Mass General Brigham. https://www.massgeneralbrigham.org/en/about/newsroom/articles/stress-in-teenagers

Blouin, M. (2022, April 15). *Research review shows self-esteem has long-term benefits.* UC Davis. https://www.ucdavis.edu/curiosity/news/research-review-shows-self-esteem-has-long-term-benefits

Bryant, J. (2022, June 23). *Most high schoolers feel pressure to make premature decisions about future.* Best Colleges. https://www.bestcolleges.com/research/students-feel-pressure-to-decide-future/

Cherry, K. (2023, November 6). *10 quick facts about social psychology.* Verywell Mind. https://www.verywellmind.com/quick-facts-about-social-psychology-2795914

Childhood nutrition facts. (n.d.). CDC. https://www.cdc.gov/healthyschools/nutrition/facts.htm

Dreher, D. (2019, June 11). *Why talking about our problems makes us feel better.* Psychology Today. https://www.psychologytoday.com/us/blog/your-personal-renaissance/201906/why-talking-about-our-problems-makes-us-feel-better

Guttman, J. (2019). *The relationship with yourself.* Psychology Today. https://www.psychologytoday.com/us/blog/sustainable-life-satisfaction/201906/the-relationship-yourself

Health benefits of having a routine. (2022). Northwestern Medicine. https://www.nm.org/healthbeat/healthy-tips/health-benefits-of-having-a-routine

Healthy and unhealthy relationships. (n.d.). Northwestern Student Affairs. https://www.northwestern.edu/care/get-info/relationship-violence/healthy-and-unhealthy-relationships.html

Healthy vs. unhealthy relationships. (n.d.). University of Washington. https://wellbeing.uw.edu/resources/healthy-vs-unhealthy-relationships/

How and why to practice self-care. (2022, March 14). Mental Health First Aid. https://www.mentalhealthfirstaid.org/2022/03/how-and-why-to-practice-self-care/

Humphry, R., & McNamara, P. (2008). *Developing everyday routines.* Taylor & Francis Online. https://www.tandfonline.com/doi/abs/10.1080/01942630802031826

Katzenstein, J. (n.d.). *Anxiety and stress in teens.* Johns Hopkins Medicine. https://www.hopkinsmedicine.org/health/conditions-and-diseases/anxiety-disorders/anxiety-and-stress-in-teens

Lenhart, A. (2015, August 6). *Teens, technology and friendships.* Pew Research Center. https://www.pewresearch.org/internet/2015/08/06/teens-technology-and-friendships/

Mandriota, M. (2022, June 30). *7 mindfulness exercises for teens and tips to get started.* Psych Central. https://psychcentral.com/health/the-benefits-of-mindfulness-meditation-for-teens

Martin, S. (2023, September 8). *8 simple ways to increase self-compassion.* Psychology Today. https://www.psychologytoday.com/us/blog/conquering-codependency/202306/8-simple-strategies-to-boost-self-compassion

Masselink, M., Oldehinkel, A., & Roekel, E. (2018). *Self-esteem in early adolescence as predictor of depressive symptoms in late adolescence and early adulthood: the mediating role of motivational and social factors.* NIH. https://www.ncbi.nlm.nih.gov/pmc/articles/PMC5878202/

Neff, M. (2023, October 19). *Helping teens develop positive friendships.* Michigan State University. https://www.canr.msu.edu/news/helping_teens_develop_positive_friendships

Ortega, S. (2022, August 16). *Gaining self-love for teen girls for overall good mental health.* Step Up for Mental Health. https://www.stepupformentalhealth.org/gaining-self-love-for-teen-girls-for-overall-good-mental-health/

Peetz, C. (2023, November 2). *Girls' self-confidence has plummeted, a new survey shows.* Education Week. https://www.edweek.org/leadership/girls-self-confidence-has-plummeted-a-new-survey-shows/2023/11

Roemer, L., Rollins, L., & Williston, S. (2015, June 3). *Mindfulness and emotion regulation.* Science Direct. https://www.sciencedirect.com/science/article/abs/pii/S2352250X15000974

Sleep in middle and high school students. (n.d.). CDC. https://www.cdc.gov/healthyschools/features/students-sleep.htm

Sparks, S. (n.d.). *Adolescent brains are works in progress.* PBS. https://www.pbs.org/wgbh/pages/frontline/shows/teenbrain/work/adolescent.html

Stress. (n.d.). Cleveland Clinic. https://my.clevelandclinic.org/health/articles/11874-stress

Strong, R. (2022, September 19). *Habits matter more than you might think - these tips can help the good ones stick.* Healthline. https://www.healthline.com/health/mental-health/why-are-habits-important

Take charge of your health: A guide for teenagers. (n.d.). NIH. https://www.niddk.nih.gov/health-information/weight-management/take-charge%20health-guide-teenagers

The teen brain: 7 things to know. (n.d.). NIH. https://www.nimh.nih.gov/health/publications/the-teen-brain-7-things-to-know

Thoele, D.G., Gunalp, C., Baran, D., Harris, J., Moss, D., Donovan, R., Li, Y., Getz, M.A. (2020). *Health care practitioners and families writing together: the three-minute mental makeover.* NIH. https://www.ncbi.nlm.nih.gov/pmc/articles/PMC6907914/

Youth physical activity guidelines toolkit. (n.d.). CDC. https://www.cdc.gov/healthyschools/physicalactivity/guidelines_backup.htm

Image References

We are grateful to Midjourney, which enabled us to create the images in this book.

www.ingramcontent.com/pod-product-compliance
Lightning Source LLC
Chambersburg PA
CBHW051421070526
44584CB00023B/3520